Classical Guitar Tunes

SONGS OF FAITH

by Owen Middleton

To access the optional online flute and cello part PDF downloads and the computer-generated audio recording go to:
WWW.MELBAY.COM/30948MEB

Grand Concert Blanca classical guitar by Pimentel Guitars, Albuquerque, New Mexico, USA.

WWW.MELBAY.COM

Preface

Like some of you, I grew up singing hymns in church, belonging to junior choir, then senior, then university and various special choruses over the years. I'm, of course, very familiar with hymns and remember dozens of them fondly.

So, when Mr. William Bay offered me the opportunity to arrange this collection of hymns that he did himself many years ago for plectrum guitar, I was happy to accept the challenge to arrange them for classic guitar and, at his direction, to not reflect his earlier arrangements at all; a creative person's ideal!

The age-old and here-to-stay method for guitar with hymns is the sing/strum idiom. Creating a solo version, however, requires the guitar to play much like a standard piano accompaniment version with voice-leading, interesting inner parts and basslines. This procedure can often offer more modern sounds than were in the sing/strum idiom; but of course, always with the most respect for the message of the hymn and with all around good taste. The interest that this effort creates may somewhat replace the appeal of a talented, interesting singer with a guitar.

It is my hope that you, the performers, will pick a few of this group and add them to your repertory, and depending on the venue, they should often be appropriate, especially if you perform in churches as I have for many years. Best of luck!

A special word of thanks to my friend, Dan Silver for his faithful proofreading of every single note in these solos! Thanks, Dan! I would also like to dedicate this volume to Mr. William Bay for his encouragement and this opportunity. Thanks, Bill!

Owen Middleton

Contents

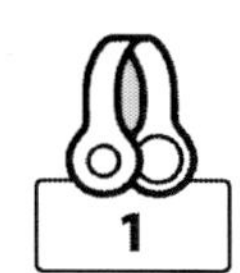

All Praise to Thee, My God, This Night
Tallis Canon

Dropped-D Tuning

arr. Owen Middleton
ASCAP

Moderately ♩ = 80

C2 C2 C3 C2 C3 C5 C5 C5 C3 C5 C7 C5 C7

rall.

C5 C7 C5 C7 ③ h.5

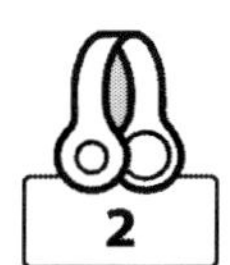

Beneath the Cross of Jesus

arr. Owen Middleton
ASCAP

Moderately ♩ = 66

Guitar

rit. *A Tempo*

rall.

1. 2.

Blessed Lord, in Thee Is Refuge

arr. Owen Middleton
ASCAP

Dropped-D Tuning

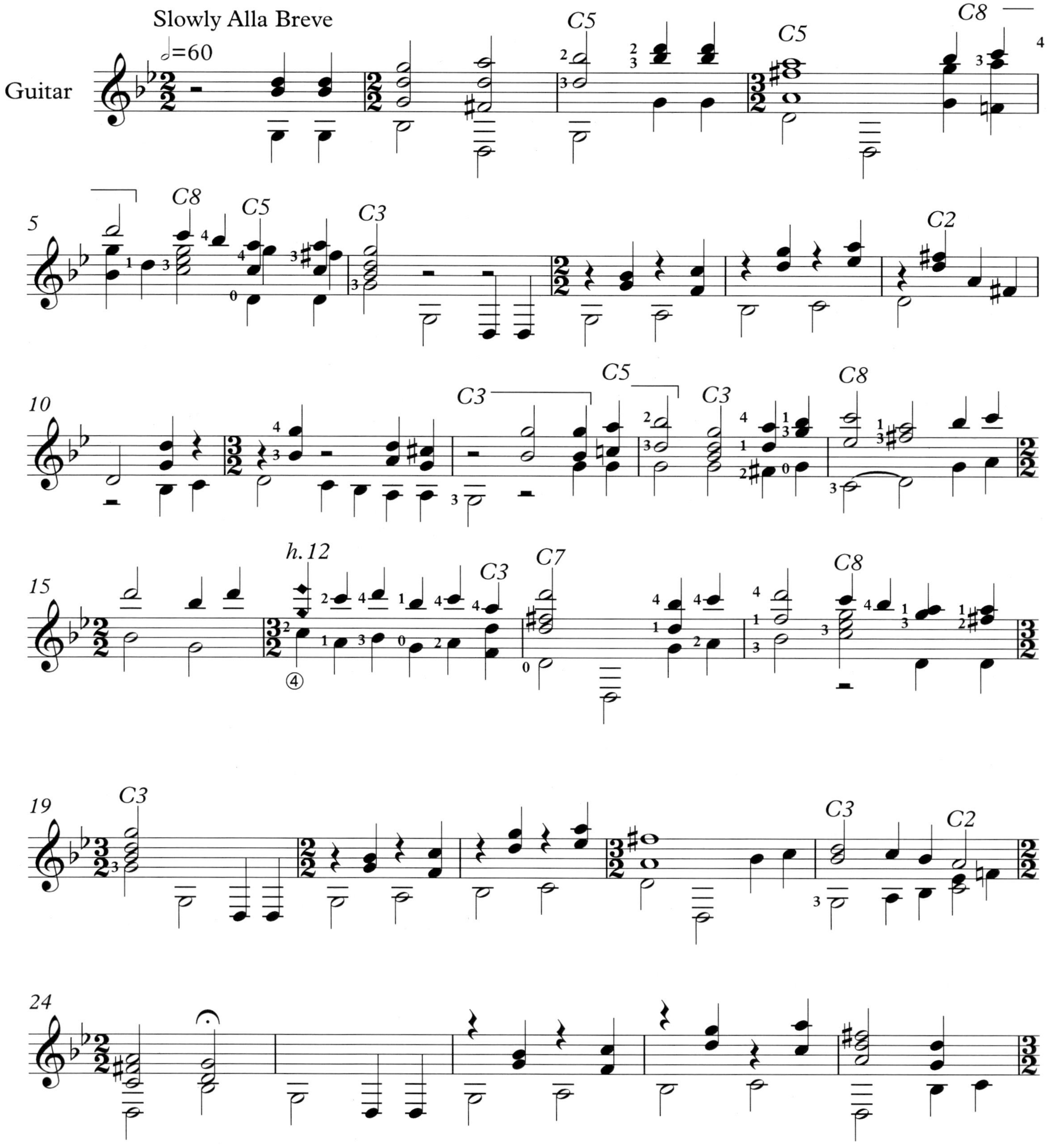

Slowly Alla Breve

29
35
C3
C8
C8
C5
41
C3
C3
C8
C3
45
h.12
C3
C8
C3

Bread of the World

arr. Owen Middleton
ASCAP

Gently ♩ = 80

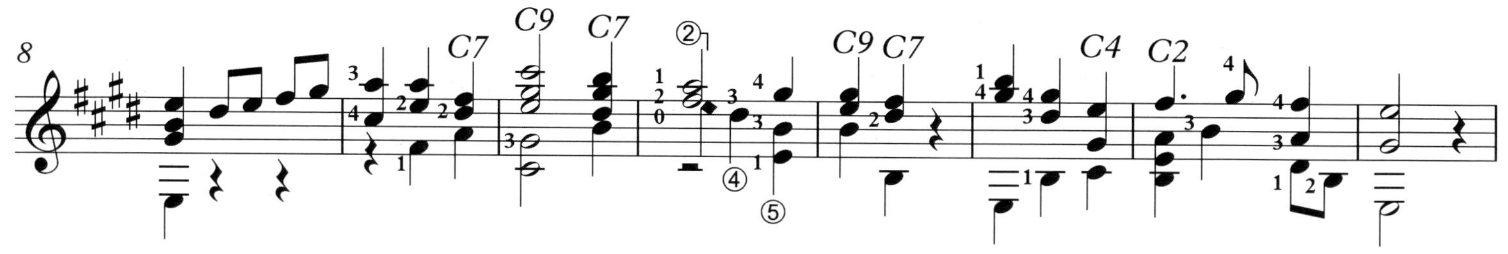

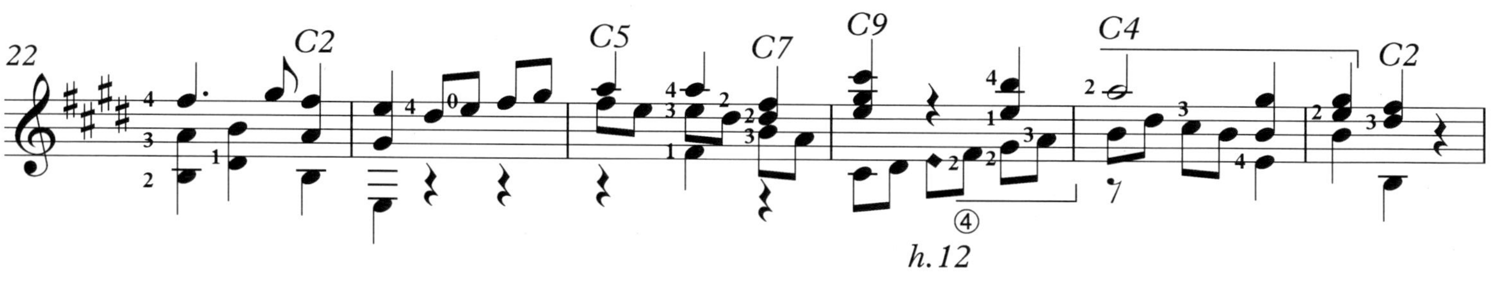

Fairest Lord Jesus

arr. Owen Middleton
ASCAP

Great Is Thy Faithfulness

Here, O My Lord, I See Thee Face to Face

How Can I Keep from Singing?

arr. Owen Middleton
ASCAP

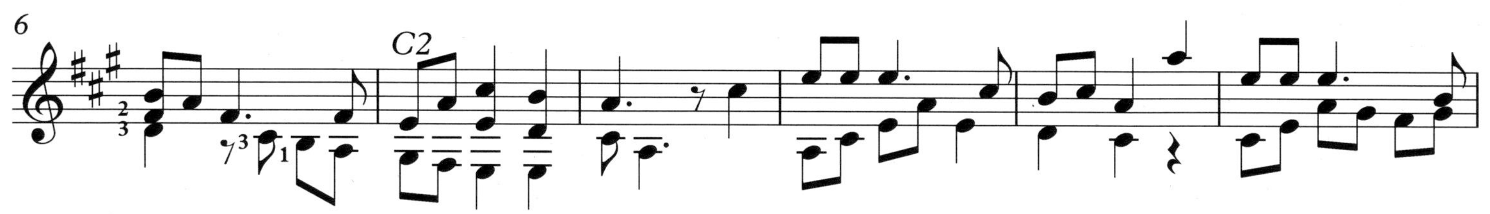

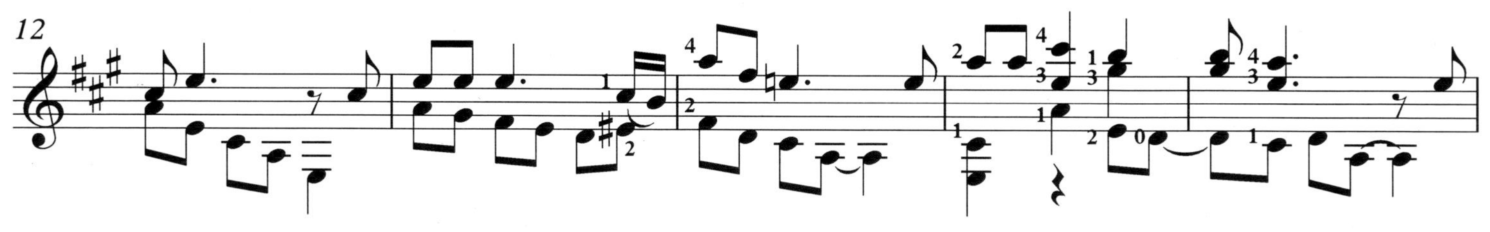

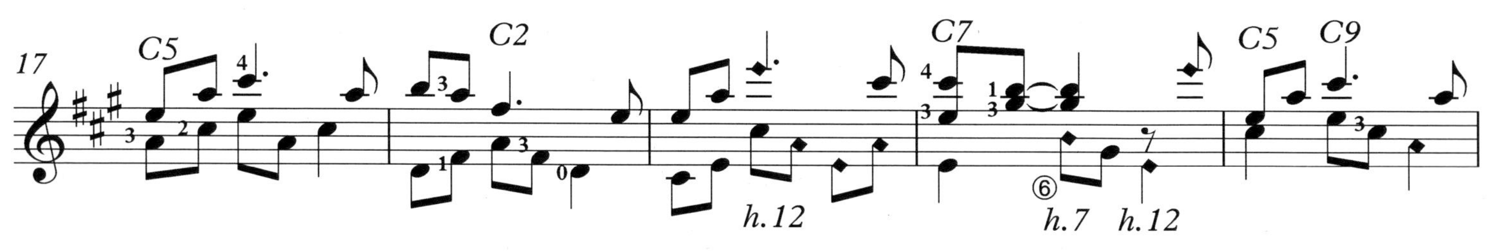

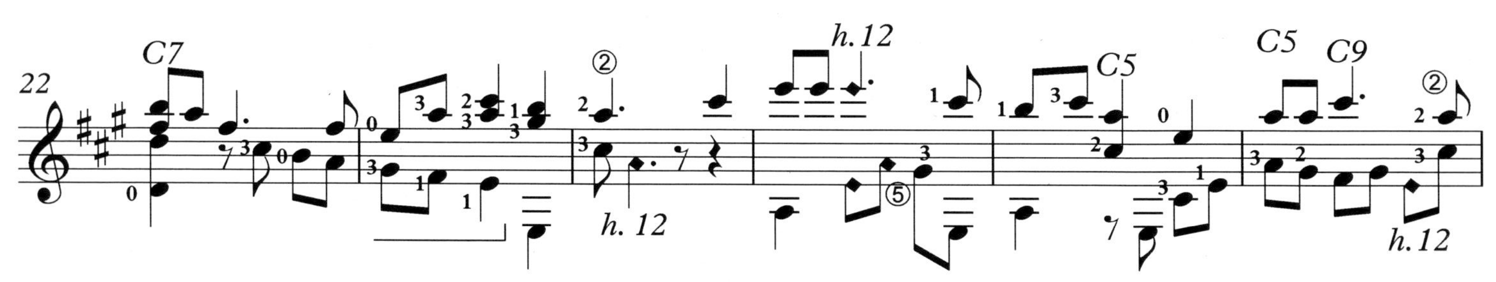

* performer to hold up hand to delay applause

Let All Mortal Flesh Keep Silence

arr. Owen Middleton
ASCAP

simile(hold C)
C5
rall.

Lift Every Voice and Sing!

arr. Owen Middleton
ASCAP

Brightly!

♩. = 76

Guitar

6

11

16

23

30

33

38
C4
43
C9
C2
C4
rall.
48
1.
2.

My Jesus, I Love Thee

arr. Owen Middleton
ASCAP

26
C5
30
34
C7
C5
39
C5
43
rall.
47
C1
C3

The National Anthem

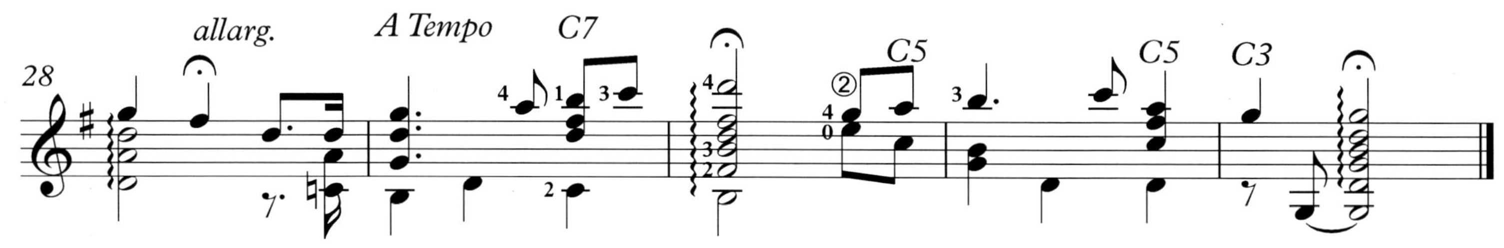

O Master, Let Me Walk with Thee

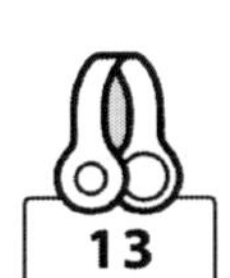

arr. Owen Middleton
ASCAP

Moderately

♩=100

Guitar

rall.

O Store Gud

arr. Owen Middleton
ASCAP

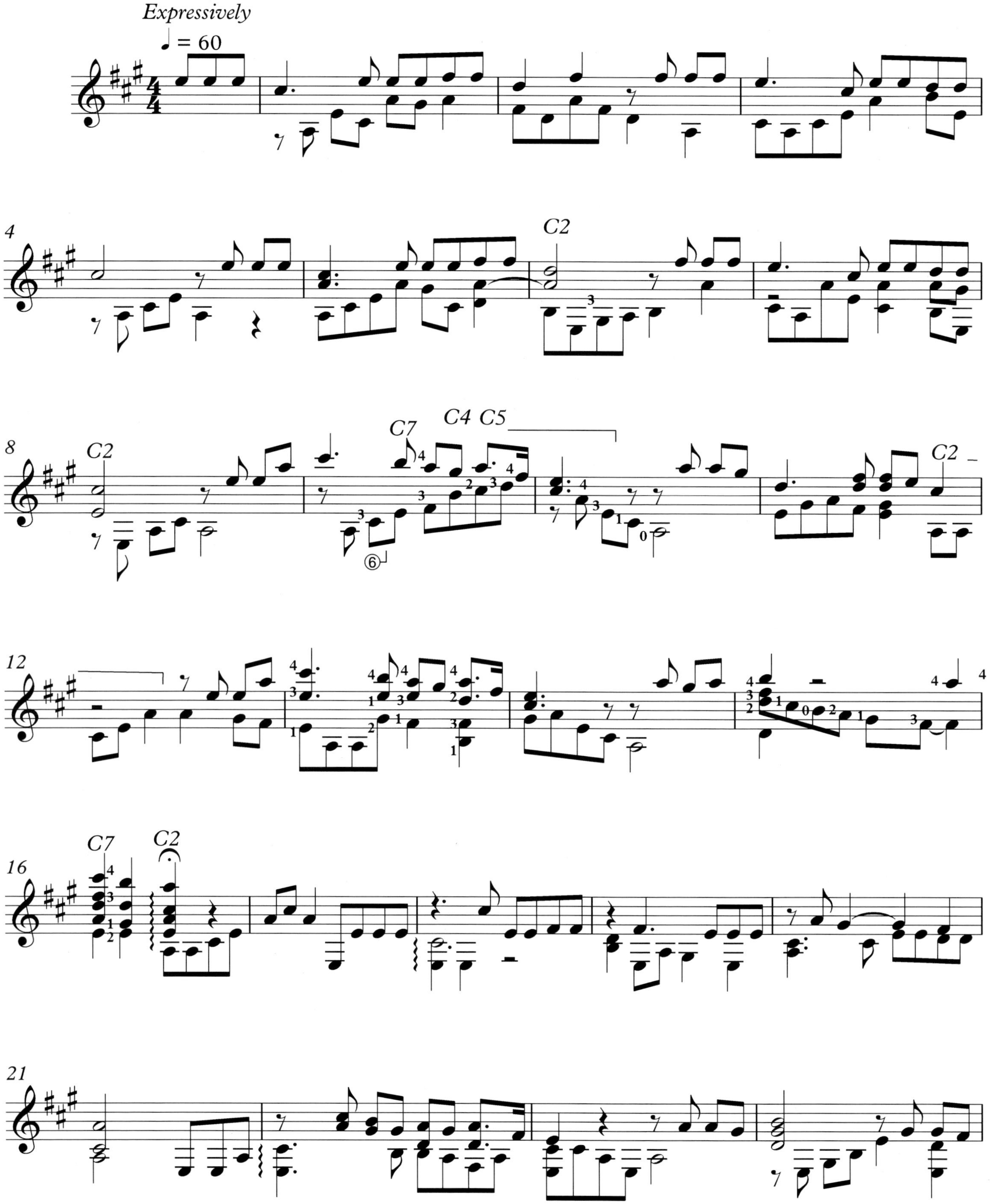

Expressively

♩ = 60

C2 C7 C4 C5 C2 C2 C7 C2

C2
C4
h.12
C2
h.12
C7 C5
rall.
C7
Poco Meno
rall.
C2
=60
C9
C5

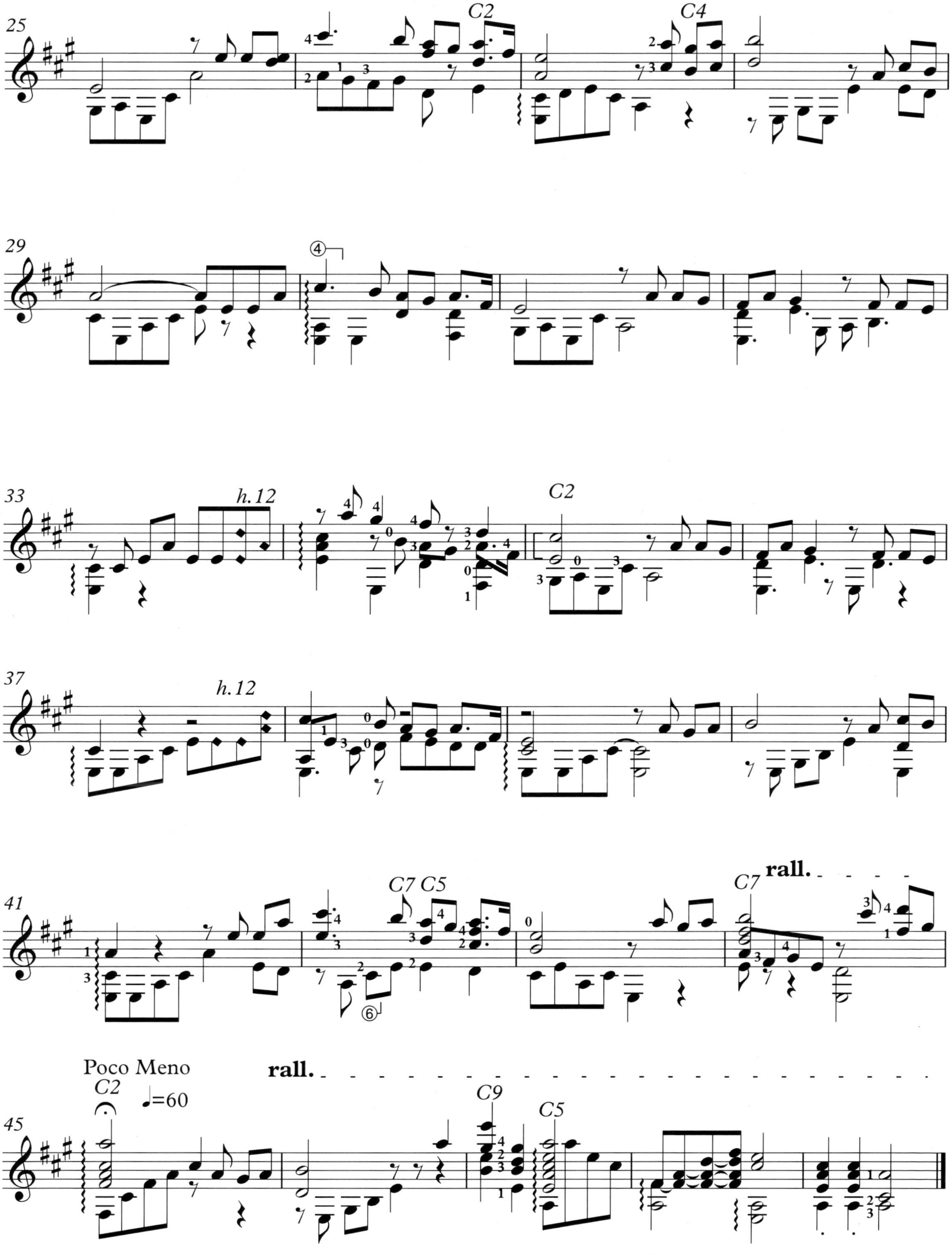

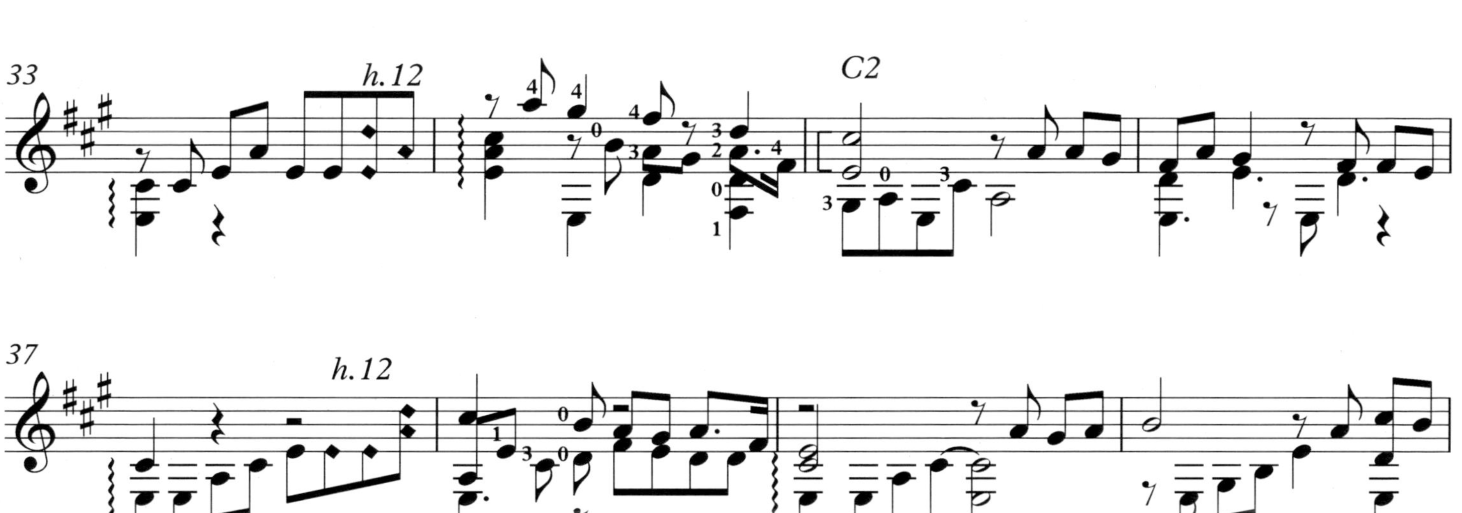

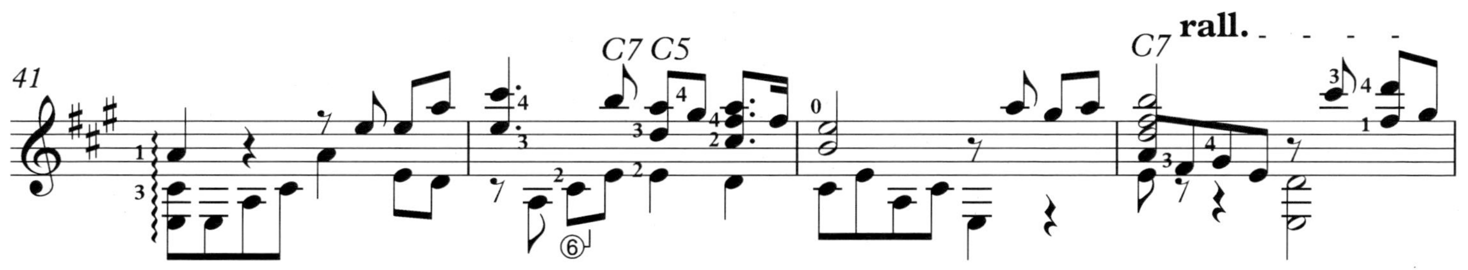

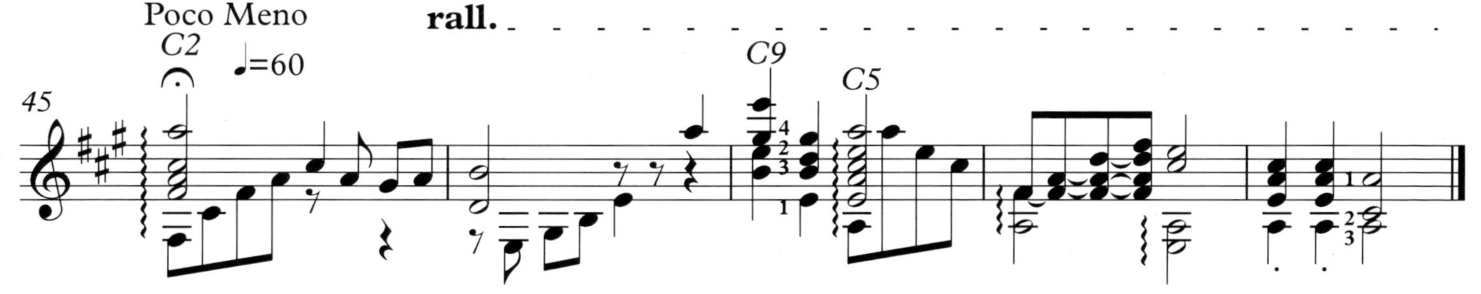

The Church's One Foundation

⑤=*G*
⑥=*D*

Steady
♩=76

arr. Owen Middleton
ASCAP

21

26
C5
C7
C8
C7

31
C5

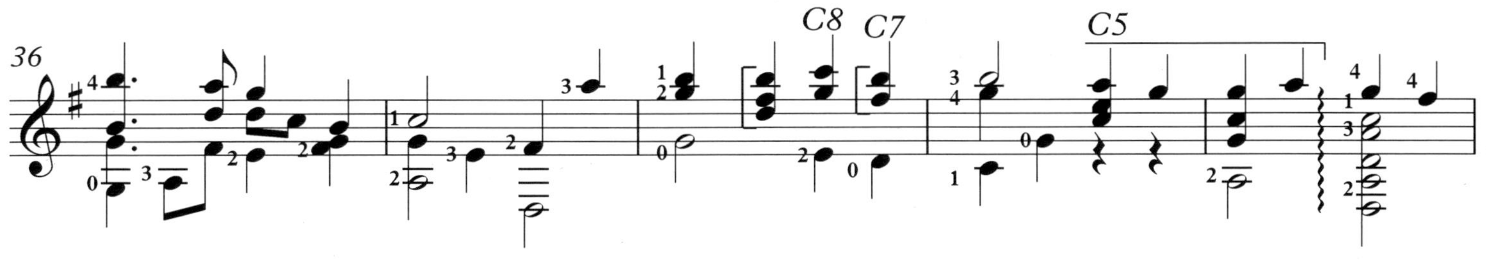
36
C8
C7
C5

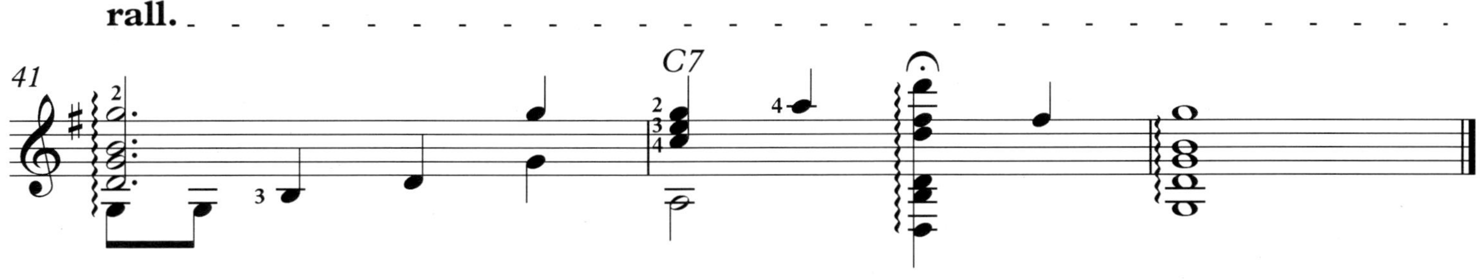
rall.
41
C7

The Church's One Foundation
Additional Arrangement

Dropped-D Tuning

arr. Owen Middleton
ASCAP

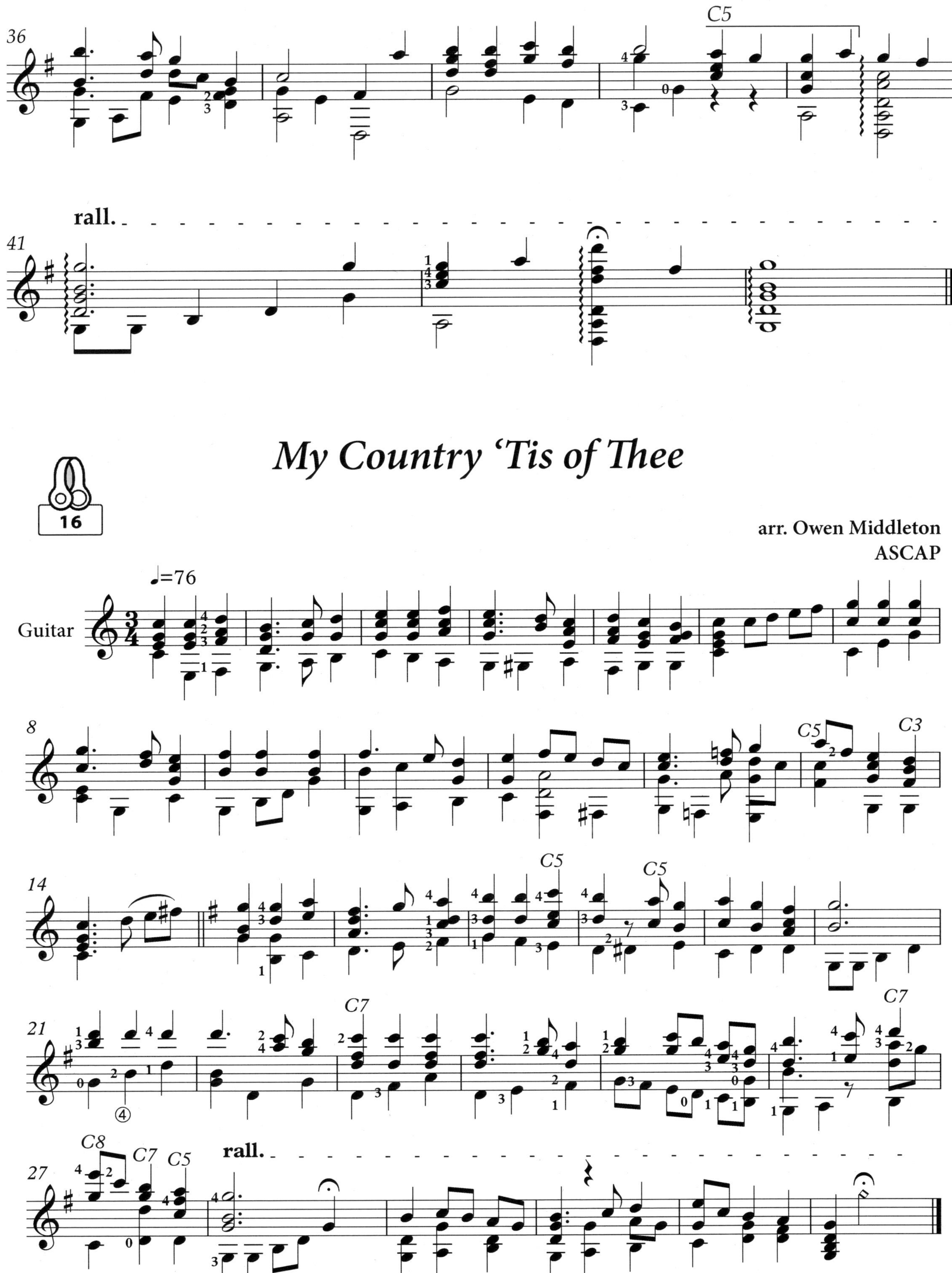
36
C5
41
rall.
My Country 'Tis of Thee
16
arr. Owen Middleton
ASCAP
♩=76
Guitar
8
C5
C3
14
C5
C5
21
C7
C7
27
C8
C7
C5
rall.

The God of Abraham Praise

17

arr. Owen Middleton
ASCAP

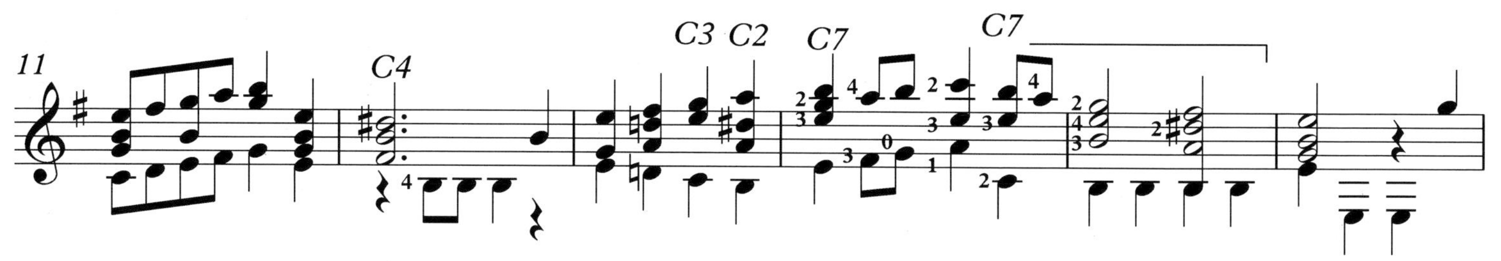

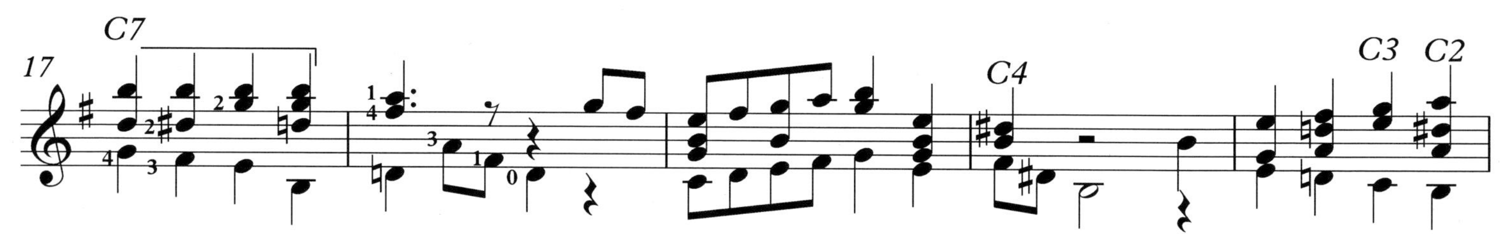

27
C1
32
C5
h.12
C5
C4
37
h.7
42
C5
h.12
C5
C4
C2
C1
47
rall.
50

Once to Every Man and Nation

18

Dropped-D Tuning

arr. Owen Middleton
ASCAP

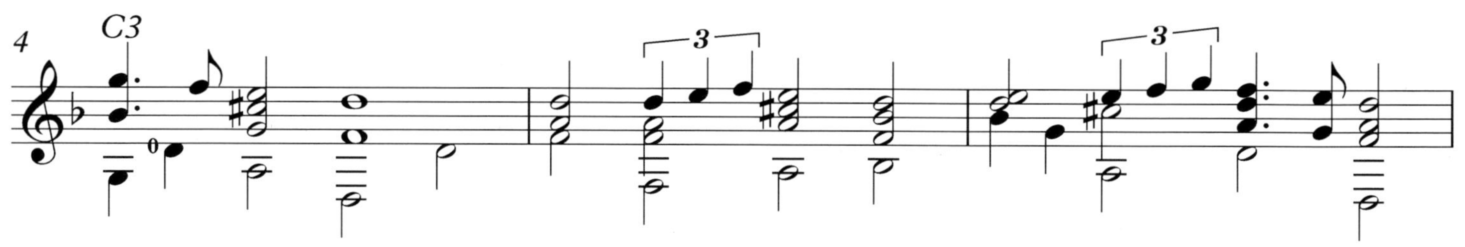

14
C5

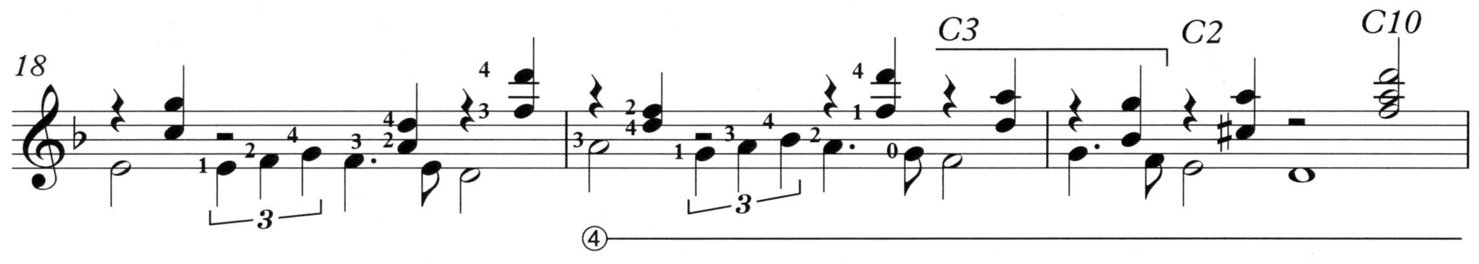
18
C3
C2
C10

21
C5
C2

24
C2
C5
C3

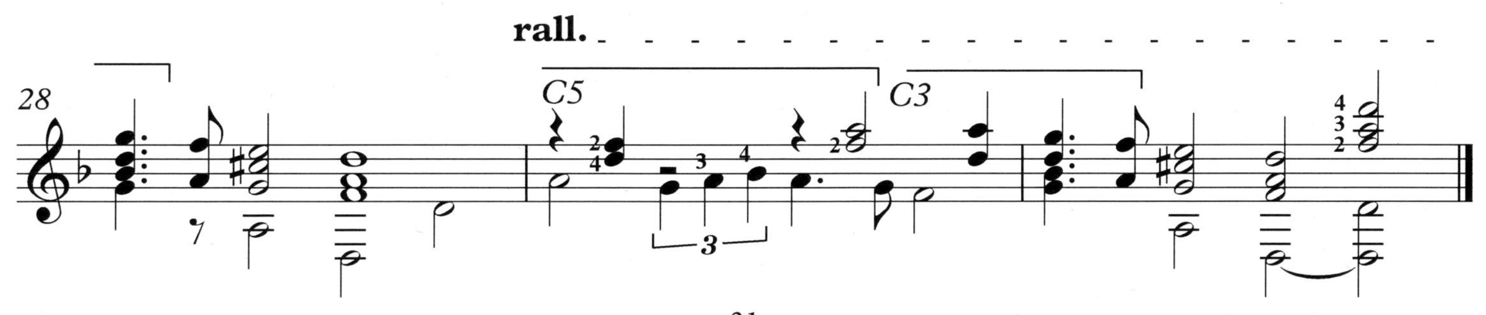
rall.
28
C5
C3

The Solid Rock

arr. Owen Middleton
ASCAP

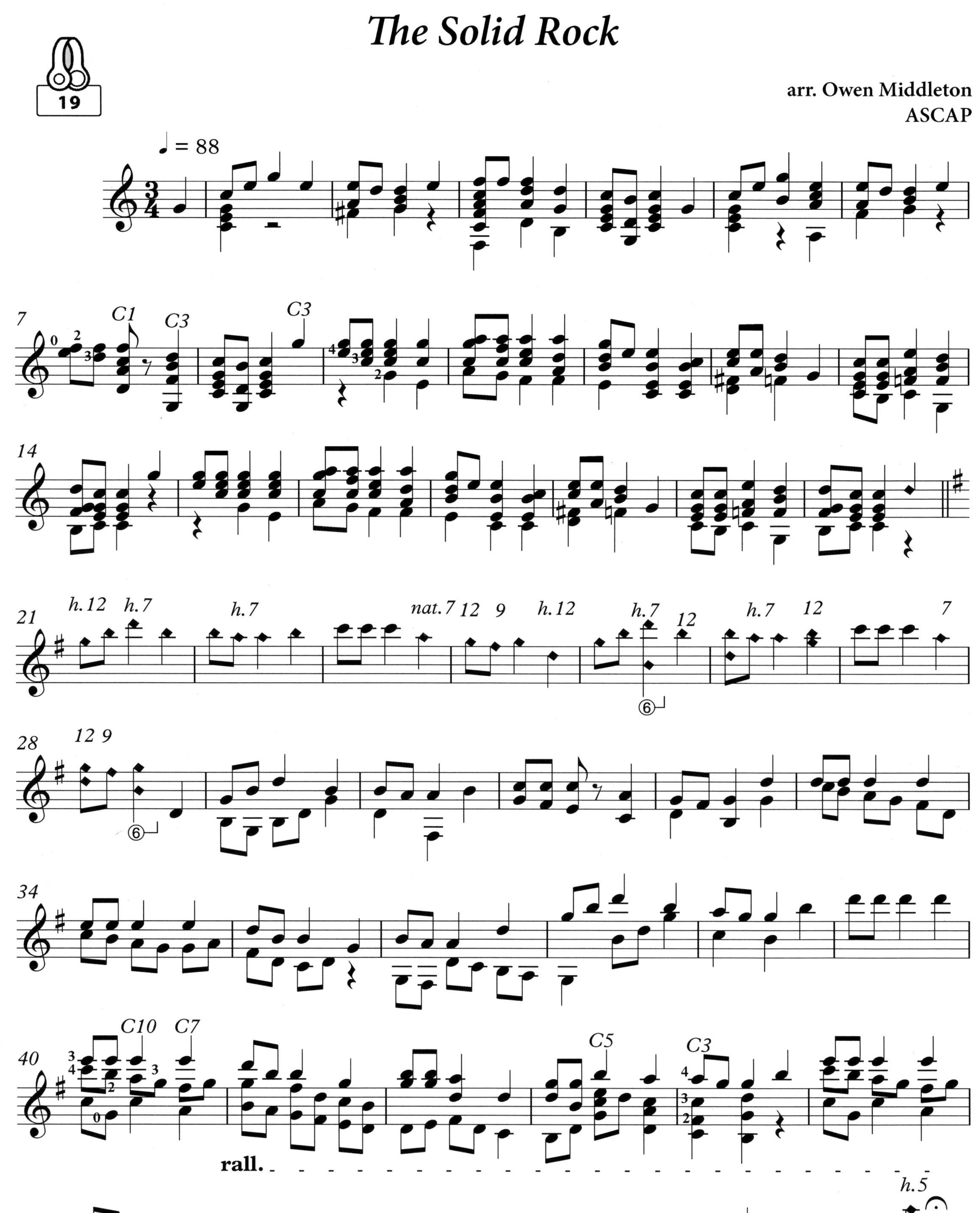

This Is My Father's World

20

arr. Owen Middleton
ASCAP

Moderate

♩=86

Guitar

C3 C1 C8 C5 C8 C7 C5 C3 C7 C3 C8 C5 C8 C5 C7 rall. C3

Watchman, Tell Us of the Night

Dropped-D Tuning

arr. Owen Middleton
ASCAP

Alla Breve
𝅗𝅥=76

espressivo

h.7 h.7 C5 h.12 h.7 h.12 C3 C5 C3 art.h.7 C2 C3

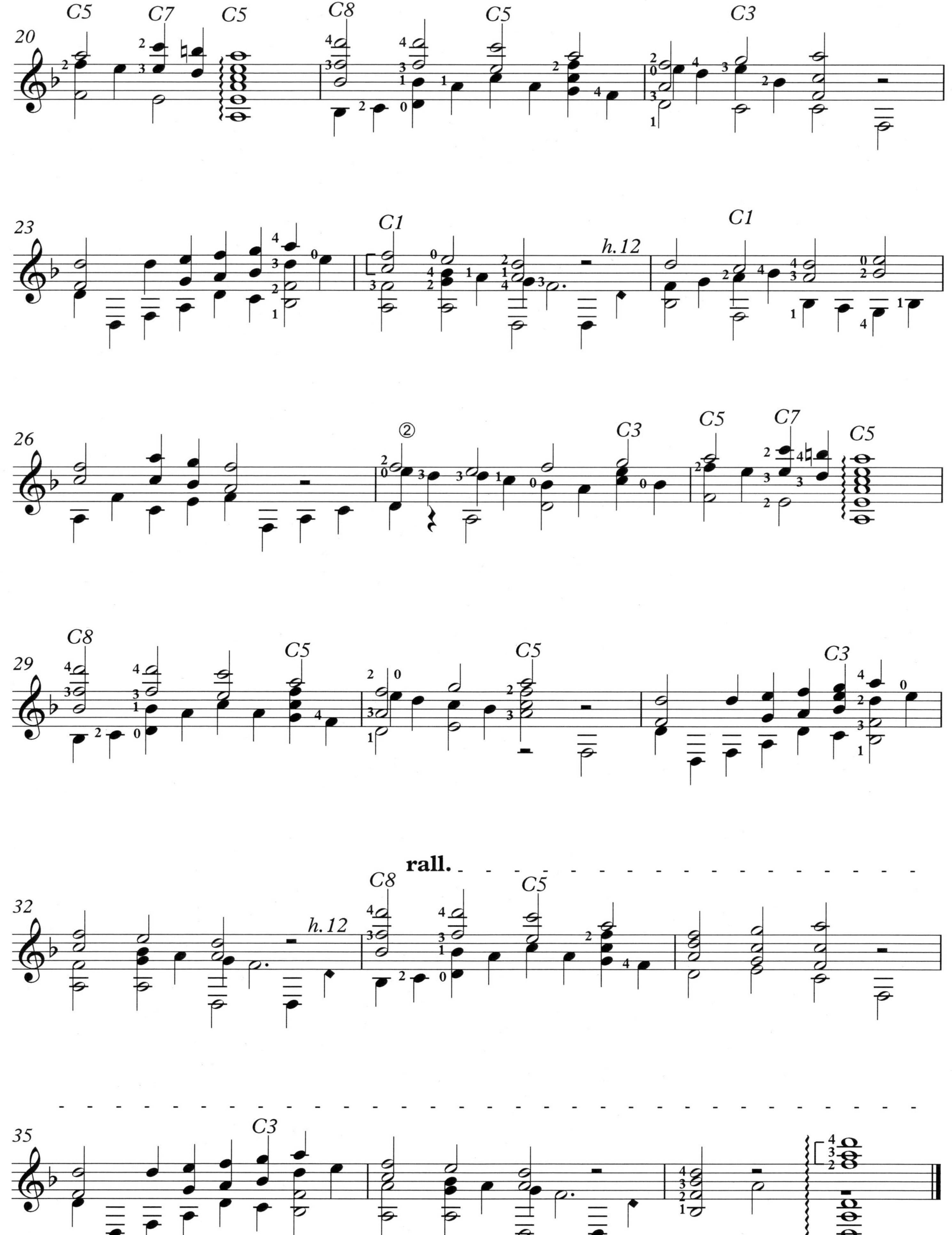
20
C5
C7
C5
C8
C5
C3
23
C1
h.12
C1
26
②
C3
C5
C7
C5
29
C8
C5
C5
C3
32
h.12
rall.
C8
C5
35
C3

About the Author

Owen Middleton
Photo Courtesy of the University of South Alabama

Owen Middleton has taught guitar for four decades. He is a published composer and author, and has performed and taught at a number of colleges and universities.

His works are performed and celebrated worldwide and are the subject of two doctoral dissertations, one by Dr. Gregory Newton at UCLA entitled "An American Original: The Guitar Music of Owen Middleton," and a second by Dr. Barton Moreau at Arizona State University entitled, "Piano Works of Owen Middleton".